HOW BURY YOUR GOODS

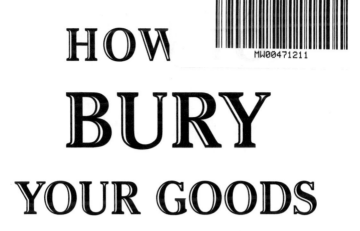

The Complete Manual of Long-Term Underground Storage
Revised Edition

eddie the wire

PALADIN PRESS • BOULDER, COLORADO

Also by Eddie the Wire:
Complete Guide to Lock Picking
Eddie's Iron
Home Workshop Professional Lock Tools

How to Bury Your Goods:
The Complete Manual of Long-Term Underground Storage
by Eddie the Wire

Copyright © 1999 by Eddie the Wire

ISBN 13: 978-1-58160-580-8
Printed in the United States of America

Published by Paladin Press, a division of
Paladin Enterprises, Inc.,
Gunbarrel Tech Center
7077 Winchester Circle
Boulder, Colorado 80301 USA
+1.303.443.7250

Direct inquiries and/or orders to the above address.

PALADIN, PALADIN PRESS, and the "horse head" design
are trademarks belonging to Paladin Enterprises and
registered in United States Patent and Trademark Office.

Visit our website at www.paladin-press.com

FOREWARD

Although all of the techniques described in this book have been field-tested and should work therefore as described, neither the Author nor the Publisher assumes any responsibility whatsoever, either real or implied, for any consequences, damages, claims or faults resulting from use or misuse of the information contained in this book. No warranty is offered, either real or implied, that any of the techniques, information, or procedures will perform to any standard stated or implied by the Author and/or Publisher, or conform to any expectations of the user.

Tough talk, huh? Well, the lawyers have ways to make your very words your own enemies, therefore, the long disclaimer. This information was assembled from reference and field research based on over 40 sources, and represents the best of the metal detector-hoarder-searcher-survivalist-guerrilla warrior minds.

This is a complete hands-on book for anyone who wants to securely package and bury just about anything. It covers location methods, site documentation, stabilizing perishables, site security, metal detector strategy, retrieval techniques, alternate hides, specifics on valuable items, and so on. All techniques are useable by the average guy or gal with a home workshop.

TABLE OF CONTENTS

WHAT DO YOU HAVE TO HIDE?

What do you have to hide? There are four classes of items:

Prohibited items, like explosives, automatic weapons, controlled substances, silencers, infernal devices, forged and altered I.D., whiskey stills, videotapes, toxic substances, chemicals, and so on.

Unobtainable-after-the-crash items, like bullets, bullet molds, primers (just try to make ten), smokeless and black powder, weapon parts, hand tools, medicines, foodstuffs, propane, reloading equipment, matches, lighters, compasses, tents, knives, sleeping bags, blankets, petroleum products, car parts (distributor caps), spare eyeglasses, stock firearms, candles, radios, or millions of other manufactured items.

Items that must remain secret, like code keys of the location of your better caches, incriminating evidence (for you and against you), Richard Nixon campaign buttons, photos, videotapes, this book, printing presses and I.D. duplicating equipment, drug processing equipment, and so on.

Items that can be easily hidden, and easily stolen, like gold and silver coinage and bar stock, stock certificates and bonds, currency of all types, T-bills, family heirlooms with market value, documents and papers, and address books. Anything small up to 50 pounds qualifies here if it is valuable.

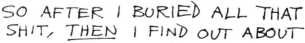

This is the short listing. Just imagine what you might not want to have around if the Imperial Storm Troopers are coming to lunch. Or imagine what you'd need if the nearest store was ten years away and the power was out. Try to make an honest list of what you presently possess that needs hiding. In the process of doing this you will also notice what you might need to get while the stores are still open. Make a list of these items also. Once you have both lists completed, arrange the items into the following groups : *ILLEGAL, UNOBTAINABLE, SECRET,* and *STEALABLE.* Now go through those four lists and try to decide if all these items are really essential enough to cache, or if they may be hidden above-ground, or just stored regularly. Put a "C", "H", or "S" by each item on the lists. While doing this you may decide that some items are not even worth the effort, so scratch these off. Also notice that "after the crash" items may be defended by the simple method of shooting everything that moves in your area — but only after the crash, not before!

After the lists are fully sorted, decide which items may be needed on short notice (like guns and ammo, and shovels, and code keys to locate the other caches), and which items may be put in more long-term storage. Even with long-term storage items, try to group these for similar needs. For example, the bullets, primers, and powder are stored together (except the primers are always stored separate from the powder) with the reloading equipment, the batteries with the flashlight, and so on. Remember too, that reloading requires some sort of building or secure space, and is not a route-of-march type of cache item.

Finally, take lists of each group of remaining items and total them up as to size and weight requirements and type of storage desired. This little bit of paperwork will save you a lot of time in the long run if you are serious about storage. After all lists are annotated, count up the number of cache sites and types of burial or storage containers required, and then change your mind now if you want, because the next step is the buying and preserving. The intelligence/resistance crowd has some good advice for us on the subject of security; always protect and segregate the smallest possible unit of whatever you are trying to hide. This means only enough team members per cell to carry out the cell's mission. This means for us that the more caches the better, the more ground between the sites the better, and so on. But remember that you are not a Case backhoe. Try to strike an acceptable balance here. There is one more list to write, because there are two types of special caches that need specific items: the bug-out cache and the defense/survival cache. The bug-out cache is composed primarily of supplies needed to travel, like gasoline, spare engine parts, tires, and so on. The defense/survival cache is useful if you are cut off for some reason from your main source of supply and need a little something to get you by until you can regain your regular supplies. The two lists should be compiled according to specific needs and processed for weight/size like the other lists.

It is worth noting that a computer program called a database could save a lot of effort in size/volume calculations, sorting, grouping, and supply you with complete documentation lists of all items, grouped by multiple headings. Consult with a Commodore user group in your area to find a "hacker" who will gladly enter your data in his/her database for a small fee. The results are worth the effort, but try to disguise the listings before you hand them over to the hacker — as stock tallies or parts inventories — for better data security on your part.

In this chapter, you have decided what to hide and how to do it. As one final step before proceeding, try this survivalist trick: Turn off the electricity for four days solid, and put a red sticker on every item you found useful during that period. Essential items get a green sticker, worthless ones a yellow sticker. List the red/green stickered items and compare to your wish list. This puts the survival question into better focus. You may even wish to attempt to retrieve a cache on the fourth day (or night) just to see if it can be done on limited resources. Perhaps you will consider burying an entire bicycle (or at least hiding one), or a gasoline cache, within easy walking distance from home, after trying this.

WHEN TO BURY IT

When to bury? All illegal items should be buried and concealed *immediately*, for obvious reasons. The next priority is secret items, then easily stolen items, finally after-the-crash items. Do not put off stockpiling and concealing after-the-crash items too long, because little things like natural disasters (floods, famine, civil unrest, tornadoes, hurricanes, drought, declaration of martial law, declaration of war) can occur with as little as 24 hours notice, and by then you are probably stuck. Eddie remembers the gasoline crisis that followed immediately after the Arab oil embargo.

"When to bury?" also refers to morning-afternoon-evening-midnight, Monday-Saturday-Sunday, spring-winter-after the first snowfall, etc. Of course, your choice of burial site will determine most of this, and the best sites are only night-accessible; more on that in chapter three. For instance, though, if winter approaches and the ground is turning to permafrost, spend some time digging several shallow caches for non-metallic items. This is simple strategy, just like not digging during the spring sog, since earth stability will ruin most attempts anyway, just ask the builders. On this same note, if you intend to have a power equipment excavation, check to make sure that county frost laws won't prevent equipment access to your site, or soft ground prevent moving around ON the site; a two-wheel backhoe is not invulnerable.

As to time of day, all things being equal, Eddie prefers midnight to six A.M. on a Sunday or Monday, since police log these as the quietest times of any patrol period.

Phase of the moon should also be taken into account, and weather forecasts from the local national weather bureau affiliate or a local planetarium will supply this information. By the way, check to see if it will be raining then, too. Fog is too freakish to be relied on (except in European locations) but makes great cover for early morning, and it also inhibits sound traveling.

WHERE TO BURY IT

There are three important points about where to bury:

(1) *SECURITY,*
(2) *ACCESSIBILITY, and*
(3) *LANDMARKS.*

Of these the trickiest is landmarking.

First of all, all humans require a focus for their actions, and anyone who desires to dig a hole and bury something usually picks a likely landmark to put it near. Treasure seekers have known this for years, and immediately search the vicinity of lawn ornaments, gazebos, old oak trees, swing sets, fenceposts, out-houses, ruined chimneys and foundations, and so on. This narrows the field of search considerably, and increases the odds of detection. It is just possible that a law enforcement group will concentrate only on areas that are *associated* with the suspect, namely you, and come up empty-handed if your cache is two farms over; but a random treasure hunter will nail your cache if it is two feet down and three feet away from the old farmers' well pit. This means that where you bury is related to when you bury, and also how and what you bury, because the type of search conducted and the equipment used will be very sophisticated if done within your own land. Random treasure hunters do not go in the field with VR detectors and depth-multipliers, and law office technicians don't use BFO loops for land searches. The type of approach and equipment likely to be used is covered in chapter six. Obvious, single, or human-made landmarks, then, should be avoided at all costs. When looking for a possible site, consider the availability of less-noticeable landmarks, like fairly distant trees that will support ropes or lines for landmarking.

Accessibility is the next consideration. The high-security sites are all at least a half-mile away from your house/land/office/stomping ground. Any plot up to twenty acres can be searched up to a depth of ten feet, depending on the size of the target buried, so your personal land is out for all but the lowest security caches. For the urban and suburban survivalist the cache should be at least ten miles from a population center like a small town, but accessible by two or three country trunkline roads, and no more than thirty or forty miles from home. Access by little-traveled roads is important in times of emergency.

Rather than waste time looking for likely spots, get copies of the topographical maps of the surrounding thirty-forty mile radius from a hiking equipment supplier, state agency, or the Dept. of the Interior. By the way, you should be familiar with orienting yourself with map and compass. The book, *Be Expert With Map And Compass,* by Bjorn Kjellstrom and published by Scribners, is typical of the field; any of the army manual reprints are also good. Get one and work some of the book exercises *before* you get stuck in the boonies. Also useful are "plat" maps showing ownership and some surveying landmarks and stadia. Real estate agents usually have these, and a county road map is also a good idea. When making notes or marks on any map do it the military way and use an overlay. Art supply stores carry clear acetate or mylar which can be taped or stapled to the entire top edge of the map, which will allow it to be folded up and down over the map. Any drawing is done on this surface with a grease pencil or marker (permanent). This also provides a measure of security since the overlay can be stored separately from the map, or a marked map used as a decoy to searchers. If you don't want to learn how to find your way (some survivalist you are) just find where you want to go on the map and where you will be, then place a straightedge over these two points and draw a line. Now using a protractor find the difference in degrees between this line and the magnetic north printed on the map and follow that heading with your compass to the desired area, then subtract (or add) 180 degrees to that heading to get back home again. Look for a forested or wilderness area under private control, rough or rocky terrain, ground *adjacent* to swamp, a little-used or full graveyard, desert, a state or county recreation area (but not a historical site), and so on. Eddie likes the graveyard best for many reasons, but it is tough to bury in unobserved. Pick at least three or four areas, check the routes to and from, and get ready for a fly-by.

Depending on your cover activity, Saturday or Sunday morning is a good bet, or anytime during the day if "land-hunting." Take the following items:

- canteen with water or whatever
- candy bar or box lunch

- insect repellant
- maps and compass and drawing material
- polaroid camera with film and lens cloth
- coveralls for underbrush penetration
- long-bladed screwdriver for probing
- camouflage netting for covering car
- 100 ft. measuring tape and mason's line
- cover activity gear (birdwatcher bird book)
- binoculars
- pack to carry all this.

As you approach each site for a cursory inspection, do a routine security check for followers by circling a county section at least one mile from your destination section. After the circle, park and look for anyone! If anyone shows, then drive away and go for the next section, following the same procedure there too. If you spot a second car, go to the third, and so on. Do the other sections on different days or later on. If you see a familiar car/plate/person, try to double them back and then follow them to find out who is so madly in love with you.

If all goes well, as you approach the first clean section note the road types on all four sides of the section, and how much discernible traffic (look for tread marks). When you go in for a bury this information is important. Also try to spot positions from which vehicular traffic can be observed *from* cover in the section. Before the bury these spots will also be important; mark all information on the maps as soon as it is gathered. If you're observed, act normal — don't eat the maps!

The circle of the section should have turned up an access road, like a farmers' tractor path, a hunting turnout, or old driveway that leads into the section *adjacent* to your target section, since people usually think occupants are in the section where the car is. If you can manage it, sometimes it is even better to park in one section, walk one section over, and end up in a third target section. Use some of these tactics now and park as far in as possible. Get out, and don't slam the door — it's a good habit to form. Cover the car with the netting, then sit with your back to a tree for ten minutes or so and take compass readings of where you are, make notes and plan a route into the area. If the site area is very large do careful planning to avoid getting lost. A triangular route with one point on the car usually is best. Soak up the sound of nothing and listen for problem noises.

Searching for a good cache spot can now begin. While moving around in the section use the rules found in the next chapter on movement to avoid detection. Try to get a feel for the land, including "dead" ground where nothing can be seen from the road. Probing with the screwdriver will disclose the type of ground; heavy clay resists digging and indicates ground water. The time of year will also give you a general indication of the fluctuation of the water table in this area. Spring is high and August is low. Loam or sandy soil is easier to dig, but easier to detect through also; although if you pick your spot right, the deep-seeking metal detectors will never suspect this place!

Will the spot be under water during a sudden torrential downpour? Will it be buried by a mudslide? Midway up a hill is good for a cache because it addresses these conditions and offers you a good vantage point while avoiding the skyline. A lack of much vegetation may indicate lots of underlying rock, so probe a lot. Will snowdrifts obliterate landmarks in winter? The local weather bureau will have information on prevailing winds that will help here. Is someone liable to build on the site? A subdivision developer's access road can go down in two days and really kink your plans!

Underlying structures, like power, gas, water, telephone, sewer and other service lines are usually associated with sides of roads, but not always. If in doubt, a BFO metal detector or some careful surveying will tell the story. Some locales even offer a line locating service for digging contractors. Take advantage of this!

Some people like to bury under or near such lines because treasure hunters avoid these areas. If you do this, avoid ground near phone junction boxes called pedestals and other junctions. Go for the long stretches.

Of course, possible landmarks are of prime importance unless you are using a "coded" cache. When you find a possible location put up a flag. In fact, don't be stingy — put up at least twenty, but know which ones are the non-decoy flags. Document all of them well as per the next section.

By the way, have you thought how many caches you need to use? Remember the rule: the more caches, the better security. In the long run, it will mean less deep digging too! When marking locations on your map overlay, try to rate the sites on a ten scale and even annotate which sites might be better for which cache types, like really heavy objects nearer an access road, and weapons accessible most easily.

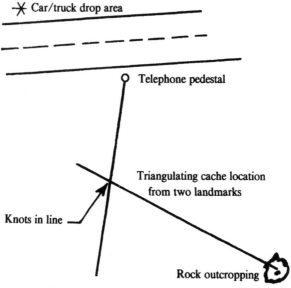

There are several ways to mark a cache site. If there are no nearby landmarks, you can look for several prominent, distant landmarks, like radio towers, grain elevators, rocky tops, railway bridges, TV aerials, power/phone poles, highway signs, and so on. By standing on one spot of ground and pointing your compass directly at each landmark in turn, a set of *bearings* can be generated, which will allow you to locate the cache with a moderate degree of accuracy. We should emphasize the *moderate* because you can still do a lot of digging with this method.

A better approach is to locate a group of four trees or non-removable landmarks and stretch a line between two, then another line between the other two such that the lines cross. Directly under this is where you should bury. With this method no measurement is necessary. Polaroid snaps and sketch maps will help to document the landmarks used.

There is an even better method. The plat maps or surveyors' maps of the county will disclose the location of so-called stadia landmarks. These are the landmarks that surveyors use to orient their surveys. Often they are located at road intersections just under the surface. Just locate them with a BFO metal detector and put a peg where it is, don't dig it up to verify it is a stadia. In addition, there will be aluminum surveyor stakes with plastic caps stamped with information numbers at the corners of each owner's lot. These are placed there during a survey, and usually must also be located with a metal detector since they are flush with the ground.

With access to two or three such *permanent* and easily documentable landmarks your cache can be very accurately located. To do this, measurements must be taken from two points to the cache, the three points forming a triangle. Since distances may be very long, use a steel tape to minimize error due to stretching. For another approach, secure a coil of music wire about .020 diameter and carefully uncoil it at home, rewinding it onto an auto rim, hose reel, 5-gallon plastic pail, or whatever. In the field, secure one end of the wire to a landmark and unroll the entire length of wire, then attach the other end of the wire to the other landmark.

Now walk to the cache site and take the two parts of the wire and twist them together with pliers several times. This harness will accurately re-locate your cache if you get the ends right, and cannot be used by someone without the right information.

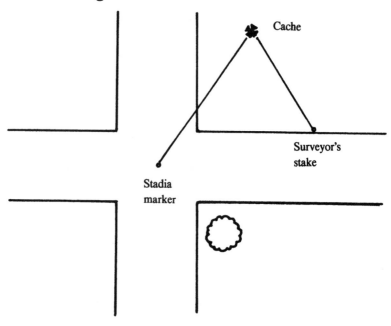

The last method of cache location is to bury flattened coffee cans at a 12-18 inch depth in a pattern you determine. These serve as artificial landmarks and may be placed very near the cache, or at some distance to increase security. Eddie recommends using a lot of these, perhaps 6-10 (they are cheap compared to pilfered AR-15's), cross-referenced two different ways; in other words, two sets. The grid that these cans outline when located with a BFO metal detector, pegged, and lined, can accurately reveal the cache location. It is unlikely that a treasure hunter would dig up each can, so with 10 cans and two grids you are fairly safe. *However,* if you need absolute security (Eddie often does; he's very insecure about insecurity) coffee cans won't do because they may all be removed or obscured. There are a couple of ways to make a permanent, non-removable marker; use salt blocks (buried) which will dissolve and mineralize the ground, or use at least two pounds of copper wire pieces cut to a half-inch length and buried one foot down over a three-foot, diameter, or use steel screws like the wire bits. Be sure to scan the ground previous to planting a non-removable coded cache marker just in case the ground is already reactive. Also, check to make sure there are no confusing naturally occurring ground features that you would mistake for a bona-fide marker. If so, then use them and document them also!

The previous edition of **How to Bury Your Goods** recommends locating a cache site by triangulating on two or more landmarks and pacing the distance or measuring, but this method, while useful, is not as good as locating a surveyor's landmark, or using a "coded" cache. If you still use this method, consider upgrading to a more accurate method and avoid a lot of needless digging and possible heart attack.

Once you have documented your cache site, mark it so it can be found in the dark during the upcoming burial, but only by you. Eddie recommends buried metal markers in a pattern that can be located with a BFO metal detector. It is wise to mark at least four dummy cache locations as well, just in case.

One more step and you are done. On the map overlay, locate your cache and then draw a rough box around the cache site at a distance of at least 200 feet. Try to locate the corners of the box at trees or recognizable places (recognizable in the dark)! These will be the points at which you place anti-intrusion devices, so choose well. Finally, get in the car and go, again checking for a tail. In the next chapter Eddie talks about the actual bury, an exercise every bit as important as any military operation.

HOW TO BURY IT

Here is a checklist of all the items you'll need to complete a secure, successful burial of your cache. Anything less may mean that you lose whatever material goods you invested.

— anti-intrusion alarms
— cloth gloves
— sharp, siliconed pick and shovel
— BFO metal detector
— flat coffee cans (if needed)
— compass
— measuring tape
— map with overlay
— sterno can and lighter
— black-out gear and outfit
— packed burial containers
— imitation skunk odor
— cruiser frame backpack
— large garbage bags or plastic sheeting
— hooded flashlight
— insect repellant
— two heavy plastic tarps 6' x 6'
— water canteen

- snack
- remove car dome light bulb
- car camouflage.

Several items here need explanation. The anti-intrusion alarms are designed to alert you to anyone coming into your position while you are burying and your attention is distracted. These devices can be as simple as jingle bells tied onto monofilament fishing line supported by forked sticks, or as complex as a pull striker igniting a flare or explosive squib. For information on booby-trap type devices see the Loompanics catalog.

A cruiser frame backpack has no sack or bag attached; it is designed to support tie-on weight, like firewood, and will be used to lug in the burial containers.

The dome light is an obvious precaution, and it is good to drive in with a dirty car, which will lower flash. Eddie recommends a coating of chainsaw oil on all shiny parts a week before the bury (check to see this does not harm car finish); this will collect dust. Rolling down all windows also reduces reflections.

All digging instruments must be sharpened with a mill file and will shed clay deposits easily if sprayed with silicone before use. The proper method of digging in difficult hardpan or clay is to use the pick/mattock to cut shallow squares in the base of the hole like a grid pattern, and these are then shoveled out and another layer is started. It goes 4" at a time this way, but is not difficult work.

A hooded flashlight has light-impenetrable material taped all over it, with only a tiny slit for light. You will be well adjusted to night vision after one hour, and it is remarkable how little light may be needed, if any at all.

The imitation skunk odor is sold for bowhunters to mask the human odor and allow a successful hunt. It comes in two parts that smell (of course) terrible when mixed. This stuff can be used liberally in your bury area, dropped as you spiral in to the cache site to prevent casual interlopers. Some brands offer a neutralizer as well.

The sterno can will serve as an effective decoy if you feel that one is needed. It can be placed at a distance of two or three hundred yards from the cache site, and once ignited, will draw attention for two hours while you dig, looking like a campfire and attracting even the most deliberate of watchers. The light will also lower an observer's night vision. Just don't put it where the heat will start a fire!

Pre-Burying Steps

The question of day vs. night burying is simple. If the bury is an especially complicated one (landmark problems) or very important, consider *only* a night burial. Even if a day burial, try for twilight or, even better, dawn. Load up all your supplies twelve hours before the departure time, especially in an urban area, or use a closed garage. To gauge the time required, figure an hour for each three feet of burying depth, and an additional two hours for security checks and incidentals.

The bury starts as the fly-by did, by observing all security precautions, even more tightly this time since your goods are on the line. During the night bury *no light at all* should show. It is easy to spot even weak sources and flashes of light at some distance if your (or somebody else's) night vision is fully active. Even glow-in-the-dark watch faces can be detected. Noise discipline is likewise important; any noisy clothing like nylon, metal hitting metal, jewelry, can give you away. Noise is also generated by walking through loose rubble and gravel, or down steep hills. If you flush a covey of birds or other wildlife, freeze instantly and move five minutes later. Remove unneeded items and tape exposed metal parts to deaden them. In quarter or greater moon phases try to tape any bright metal to eliminate flash. While walking around in the boonies stay in the soft ground, the non-crunchy area, and close to the tree lines. Stay within or near the large clumps of vegetation and definitely avoid "skylining" yourself by walking over the bare crest of any hill or rise. If necessary, make a great detour to avoid this because it is so easy to spot movement in this manner. Avoid tracks, so avoid walking through sand or mud, and if you are traveling through tall grass (excellent cover) zig-zag direction every few yards because a straight line through grass is a giveaway as to direction, and easily found. Always drive completely around the site and observe where the tire tracks are, trying to stay in these, and stopping on the road that you used for parking/storage last time, in the section *adjoining* the cache site section. After stopping, immediately get out and (don't slam) cover the car. Now load up and proceed across the road to the point you marked where vehicle traffic can be observed. Cross the road where cover is close to both sides of the road, or where the ground dips low, or the road curves.

Observe for at least one-half hour, your night vision will get better as you sit there. Also, listen for anything out of the unusual; if you can, smell the air. Anything that will help you to find out if you are alone or not. When you are satisfied, move. Eddie likes to walk in the furrows of a plowed field since it hides tracks well; try it! Deploy any location harness you may have, if it requires anchoring to survey landmarks located at the road edge, and proceed to the box area to set your decoy sterno fire, anti-intrusion traps and lay the skunk oil if you wish. Stop often and listen. Finally, proceed to the burial site, locate the cache site if you left markers, and begin to dig.

The plastic tarp is used to keep "crumbs" of earth from remaining to give away your cache location. *All* earth must be deposited on the tarp and either replaced or carried a long distance from the cache site. If the surface is turf or some other surface material, it is wise to initially cut a plug with the shovel blade and lift it out whole. It will be replaced after the bury, and then watered with the canteen contents, which will help to re-establish the root system and hide evidence of tampering.

Dig and listen in shifts, which will keep you rested as well. Once the required depth is reached (know how long your shovel handle is), stop digging and make another sweep of the perimeter, looking, listening, and sniffing!

These may seem like elaborate precautions, but in Eddie's neck of the woods night hunters and poachers are common, many are "clued in" to survivalist burying, and all are curious! How much would it cost to replace your cache in terms of money and time already invested?

If all is clear, return to the cache and line the hole with the garbage bag material, which will prevent the earth from gripping the container strongly and making removal difficult. In fact, for insulation from the ground, which aids in detector foxing, some people lay down a box of styrofoam house insulation in the hole. Now "plant" your container, then bury by packing earth tightly around the container, every few inches, in layers, as you fill the hole.

If you intend to use a decoy, plant this at least eighteen inches above your cache container, and finally re-insert the plug, water it, and pick up any excess dirt in the tarp. Carry (do not drag) the excess away, and look for any evidence of your passage, like tracks, broken under-brush, or whatever! Try to repair as much of this as possible.

At the first stop to remove the anti-intrusion alarms, scatter the extra earth. Retrieve all of your equipment (count the pieces) and hike back to within fifty yards of your car. Then halt to listen once more. If you are suspicious, try throwing a few pebbles in the suspect direction to get a reaction. The last step is loading up, starting up, and driving away, remembering to stay in the tracks if possible, and using parking lights the first few hundred yards.

HOW TO PACK BURIAL CONTAINERS

Packing requires attention to several considerations:

- Neutralizing air in container
- Preservation of contents
- Padding of contents
- "Sanitizing" contents (no fingerprints)
- Matching container to contents
- Correctly sealing container
- Coding container.

How to manufacture and/or select containers will be discussed elsewhere. This chapter covers packing only, and first comes preservation. What is being packed? How much does it cost? Is it expendable? It is not necessary to expend a lot of time on packing bulk items like food, and water, but guns and ammunition require far different handling. Eddie wraps a handgun, but not a bottle of aspirin.

The first thing to consider during handling is "sanitizing" the contents. If worst comes to worst and your cache is discovered, there should be no nametags, fingerprints, serial numbers, or anything that can be connected to you or your activities. This means taking a good look at *all* of your goods and acting accordingly.

In addition, any thick coating must be handled with gloves.

If you must file serial numbers, be sure to stamp *over* the real numbers with a bogus serial, *then* file them both off! The stresses produced in the underlying metal during stamping can be recreated with special techniques, so the double-stamping disguises the true number. In security slang it's called a mask. I should also mention that a good cover story to explain the sudden absence of your beloved gun collection will divert attention and suspicion away from any burying activity. Tell people you sold it. In addition, don't mention anything about the real need to bury things to protect them from search and seizure! One "hiding place" building book said it all when it advised to put the book in your very first hidey hole, to prevent suspicion. The information security chapter should also be consulted for ways to encode your site documentation, because anything seized in a warrant search is fair game. A combination found in the desk can be used to open a vault if it lies in an area associated with you. A key can be used also, which is why people carry those little metal boxes with combination locks in their cars and *memorize* the combination because then it may not be forced open in a vehicle search, only if a warrant is obtained. This may vary in your jurisdiction, however.

Now to the strategy of packing: what goes where and with what? Imagine yourself at midnight in the freezing rain, hands cut and numb, digging up a package. How would you like it packed? Try to package each item separately for easy carrying and double protection; it beats breaking up large bundles in the rain! Any items like broken-down rifles should be packed individually, then all items double wrapped together. Nothing is more useless than a rifle without a bolt group.

All packaging should be labeled clearly. Eddie prefers a laminated tag attached with florist's wire or a stick-on Avery label (available in many sizes). Color coding can be added for quick decisions. Also, each package should have the ready means for opening it attached to the package. Buy a box of one hundred single-edge razor blades and tape one to each package with filament strapping tape.

Obviously ferrous (iron- or steel-based) materials must receive special handling. The worst thing to do is spray on a coat of anything! The spray can release extremely cold contents as a result of the gas expanding, and the cold will condense water in the air and trap it *between* the metal and the oil, which causes deep rust pitting. There is a better way.

OF COURSE, IF I DIP THE TRACTOR IN HOT COSMOLINE FIRST, I HAVE TO BURY IT BY HAND.

The method of choice is cosmoline, a thick grease available from many survival/military surplus outlets. A good substitute is vaseline or a vaseline/paraffin/beeswax combination. Hot dipping requires a container as large as the largest part to be treated, which is usually a gun barrel, so consider using a PVC pipe container for dipping. To heat such a container run a piece of copper tubing down to the bottom and back up out the top and run very hot water through the tube. The resultant temperature will not exceed 200 degrees. The metal must be solvent cleaned before dipping; use gloves during this whole procedure. Pre-heat the metal before dipping, to dry it out, by holding it under a heat lamp. In fact, the entire room should be at least 70 degrees while working. The metal should be dipped at least ten minutes, then removed and hung up. When cold it must be wrapped in plastic sheeting or aluminum foil to prevent messy handling.

If dipping is too much work for a few items, cosmoline can be heated and brushed on (pre-heat the metal as before) but don't allow the cosmoline to be heated over 300 degrees — it is flammable.

Remember to pack a bottle of solvent, a brush, and some rags in each container that holds cosmoline preserved metal. A preserved weapon must be thoroughly cleaned, especially the bore, before firing. A trace of excess grease will cause an exploding weapon, never any fun!

Other coatings for metal exist, like WD-40, 1ps-1, and other such clones. Just remember to spray onto a rag, then wipe onto the item. Very small items may be grease or oil packed. Machinists prevent corrosion of fine metal by storing all such items in quart cans of motor oil. Linseed oil or cup grease may also be wiped on for protection. Any wiped items should be wrapped in plastic sheeting.

Before Eddie leaves the preservation of guns, a couple of other things need mentioning. During the retrieval process you many not have the ideal conditions of security, concealment, weather, health, and so on, that you wish for. Eddie has a *good* strategy for weapons burial: bury one small weapons cache in a very easy to find and easy to get to location (even if it means lowering security standards a little) and pack it as follows. Use an unscrewable PVC container with the top wrench packed outside the pipe. First item in is a twelve gauge shotgun *loaded* with BB shot. This gun must be ready to shoot instantly (not broken down) — but not cocked. To pack it, clean the weapon three times over a thirty day period. This is because much-used weapons develop hairline faults in the receiver and barrel that "hoard" combustion by-products and leak them out a little at a time. The repeated cleaning will catch these traces. With the gun cleaned, unoiled, uncocked, and loaded, put it into a large plastic sleeve improvised from a thick painter's poly drop cloth, and displace the air in the envelope with inert gas as described elsewhere, then seal the envelope. Now put a double wrapping on and seal. Finally, put a piece of fluorescent colored tape just behind the trigger group on the stock like a bag tie, and one in front of the trigger guard. The whole idea is to be armed in the least time possible. That may be very important someday! The rest of the container contains only fifty rounds of ammunition in various loads (buckshot, quail shot, slugs, and so on). Try not to put other survival gear in this container. The *more* essential containers you bury, the greater your compartmentization (as the intelligence crowd says) and the less your loss if one container is compromised (uncovered by strangers). This rule is repeated elsewhere and for good reason. By the way, if you are packing ammunition components, like primers, powder, bullets, or cases, always leave them in their original packaging, and preserve on top of that. Primers in particular are packed for low moisture exposure, low dust scatter, and such that if one fires the rest will not go off systematically. Heard the one about the guy who dumped primers into a glass mason jar? Eventually trace dust adhering to the primer body all sifted to the bottom, he set the jar down hard, the dust detonated, and all the primers "zippered" or detonated each other like a nuclear fission reaction. He lost a hand; you could lose a cache. It should also be noted that loaded rounds of ammunition, unless they are specifically preserved like all government-spec. ammo, will be ruined by any application of petroleum-based solvents and/or oils.

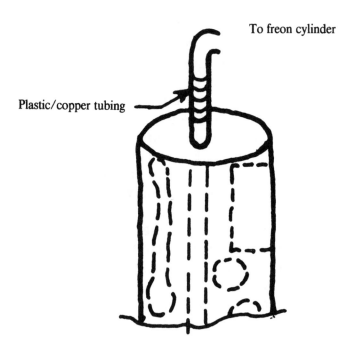

To freon cylinder

Plastic/copper tubing

Bagging is the easiest method for most other items. The commercially available heat sealers and bags designed for leftover food storage are excellent for this purpose. Also available are zip-lock and sandwich bags, if air-tightness is not at issue. For any thin-film sealing, all protruding or sharp edges must be padded or taped. To exclude air from individual bags or fully packed containers, fill the space with some padding. Eddie recommends crumbled styrofoam bead board or blue house construction insulation board. Styrofoam pellets in lots of shapes are available to bulk out a container. Hand squeezing also helps for bags. For production work it is possible to hook up a ¼" hose to the end of the vacuum cleaner nozzle with tape, and use it to draw out excess air!

To displace air in larger containers, some kind of inert gas can be used. To do this insert a ⅛" diameter copper tube to the bottom of the container, and arrange to pipe in a gas like freon (used in automotive air conditioning service) or carbon dioxide. Carbon dioxide can be generated in a garbage bag by mixing vinegar and sodium bicarbonate and piping it in, but this gas is moist. Eddie prefers a couple of chunks of dry ice thrown in the bottom just prior to packing. To verify that the container is gas-filled hold a lighted match over the container mouth, and if it snuffs out, cap the container quickly.

Fiberglass packing is good for non-container burial. Auto body suppliers carry small repair kits consisting of glass cloth, resin, and hardener. The item is wrapped in the cloth and then liberally coated with the resin/hardener mix using the proportions listed on the container. Acetone may be added sparingly to make the mix a little more liquid. This material will heat up as it hardens, so avoid packing ammunition in this manner unless it is well insulated and chilled. Once the epoxy hardens, it is ready to bury. Eddie packs a hacksaw blade with a sharpened point outside each fiberglass-wrapped package to aid in opening.

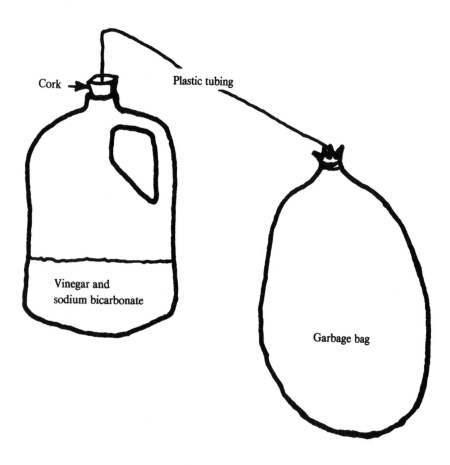

Cork

Plastic tubing

Vinegar and
sodium bicarbonate

Garbage bag

For really tiny objects, freezing/canning plastic containers are ideal and better than mason jars, which may be broken if not well padded. Pill bottles are also excellent and airtight also.

One other coating for metal is useful. It goes under different names, but it is a dippable, solvented plastic used to coat tool handles.

Moisture in the air of the container will cause serious problems. Even if the container is totally dry, moisture may creep in due to the presence of ground water under pressure, so some extra insurance is in order. A desiccant is a chemical that attracts and bonds to water. Three on the market are useful: ANHYDROUS CALCIUM SULFATE, SILICA GEL, and VP PAPER. Some of these are "indicating." This means they change color according to the amount of water absorbed. The first two can be reactivated by heating to drive off the water. When packing make sure the chemicals are as dry as possible.

Both chemicals are used in the laboratory and are thus available from the lab suppliers in both prepackaged forms (container with air holes) and in bulk. If you decide to buy in bulk, Eddie recommends packaging by weight in an improvised cloth bag with a wraptie to close the top. The survival/gun dealer suppliers also sell small, paper, laminated packages of silica gel also, but the average container may need two or more of these for adequate protection. All permeable dryer envelopes must be segregated from actual contact with any metal. This is necessary since the chemical becomes corrosive as it absorbs water. The best way to do this seems to be a plastic pill bottle with a lot of holes in it. Eddies uses a red-hot awl point to cut these holes. Remember that desiccants are not a substitute for proper packaging procedures, and they cannot handle any water leakage into the container, they only dry out what's inside. For this reason, don't use desiccants in containers with paper; it will be decomposed by the *lack* of water. Inadvertently, Eddie discovered that Japanese pianos are sealed with three one-pound bags of silica gel before export; a piano dealer could make your day! Silica gel is also available from the craft supply shops; it is used for drying flowers, and making apple-head dolls!

Padding the individual packages is next on the list. If you are using styrofoam to displace air, this will do nicely, but there are many substitutes. Tampons, plastic "bubble" sheet (in fact, any commercially available packing), rags, wadded newspaper, salvation army clothing (bought in bulk and useful in a survival situation), dry sawdust, cardboard, and on and on. Pack a layer at a time and shake together before packing the next layer. For many small items, the print shops and offices have small vibrating tables to stack paper, and one of these could serve you well. Halfway through the pack, insert a dryer package. After packing, but before filling with inert gas and sealing, put a list of the contents on the top.

If you are using screw-on tops, put a sealant on the threaded parts before screwing together, for a nice airtight lock. Teflon tape, caulking, and pipe dope, all work well. After the container is sealed, wait for any adhesive to dry, then do the final test; *immerse* the container in water and look for bubble trails. Check for at least a half hour. This may sound extreme to you, but water under ground can build up considerable pressure, so better a packing job ruined in the bathtub than underground a month before you un-bury it.

Finally, code the container to indicate it's contents. Eddie uses a vibrating, security-type etcher which marks everything well, and can be identified by touch if large areas are roughed-up in a pre-arranged code. As a final touch, strap two sharpened hacksaw blades, inside a triple bag, to the container with heavy cord. This can be a lifesaver in a desperate situation.

OUTFOXING THE SEARCH TEAMS

Metal detectors are used in many areas of law enforcement now, and the technology is advancing rapidly. For instance, metal detectors are now tailored to different tasks, like house wall searching, walk-through metal detecting, hand-held detecting, deep ground searching, and water searching; each device is targeted to its task.

The state-of-the-art equipment for deep ground searching has sensitivity that is, of course, related to type and profile of target, but cases of auto engine blocks being detected at ten feet deep show you what a search team is capable of. Let's examine the theory of detecting, and then look at ways to exploit the weakness of a deep search system.

All detectors send out an energy field similar to radio waves. The shape of the sweeping coil makes the shape of the field resemble a cone, and where the hole would be is the most sensitive area of the field. The field reacts to any conductive substance, usually metal, but also mineral deposits, and even salty wet ground. The degree of response is based on the relative conductivity (copper is a better conductor than iron, so it shows up better on the detector), and the surface area presented to the field. A piece of aluminum foil spread out and buried a foot down is easily picked up, but the same foil crumpled together and buried eight inches down might be missed; even though the mass is the same, the surface area is much smaller.

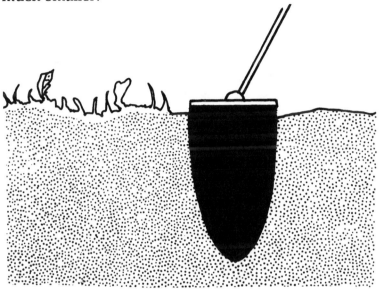

The cone-shaped field emitted by a metal dector.

Another factor affecting response is distance from the coil. Since air is a poor conductor of electricity, if the search coil is one half inch off the ground, the effectiveness is reduced thirty per cent or more. Also, the more moisture in the soil, the greater the conductivity between soil and metal, which shows up as well. Some World War Two guerrillas fought this by packing metal in a series of insulating wooden boxes; if the soil can't electrically connect with the metal, efficiency of the detector decreases.

The problem then, is to provide:

● maximum depth
● minimum target area presented to coil

- lowest conductivity
- confusing shielding
- red herrings
- camouflage.

The maximum depth part is self-explanatory, but many people skimp here. Eddie recommends the use of commercially available earth augers or post hole diggers to aid in small object burial, or PVC container caching.

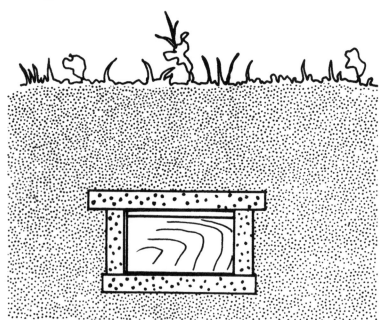

Wooden containers reduce conductivity and lower the chance of detection.

Minimum target area is related to depth. It is heart- and back-breaking to bury your rifle canisters end up, but nothing shows up with a more distinctive signal than a long, sideways, metallic object. Seen on its side, a gun has a surface area of almost a square foot, while on its end it is no bigger than a quarter if muzzle up.

Lowest conductivity means that the more metallic objects should be buried deeper, and in drier soil if possible, and never in metal containers. It should be noted that some law enforcement agencies will also use a disturbance detector if they suspect a good bury or a non-metallic mass like documents that will not register on a metal detector. The disturbance indicators operate like little sonar units and register drastic differences in the soil continuity, so non-metallic is no guarantee. However, if you are making wooden boxes to store things in, don't use nails; try dowels or hot glue.

Confusing shielding is where the strategy starts. People bury things in the first place to avoid detection, to avoid the knowledge that something is there, because secrecy is your best and *only* defense. In light of the advanced capacity of modern metal detectors it is only wise to bury far away from your homestead and increase the amount of square footage that must be searched. Eventually it will be impossible or impractical to cover all suspect ground. To repeat, *do not attempt to decoy a deep-seeking metal detector.* Such machines have operational modes that actually ignore things like pennies and mineralized soil, and in the hands of an expert, will eventually find your cache.

The problem with a deep-seeker is that with the increased sensitivity comes many more false signals per six inch sweep of the coil, so the search proceeds much more *slowly.* The deeper pattern (an inverted cone shape) also means that significant overlap must be maintained to insure full coverage. Perhaps even a twenty acre plot can be searched in this way, but not a fifty, hundred, or section-sized area.

Let's say, however, that you are up against an amateur with a more regulation type of detector, or you have a limited area to bury in, or you just want to cause as much hassle as possible in the hope that they'll give up quick. Here are some expert methods of confusion (this means the experts will hate you for doing this).

Detector operators soon learn to distinguish probable depth and type of object by the amount of rise and fall in the audio signal, and its duration. There are only a few objects that are commonly encountered, like pennies, pull tabs, and can lids, and the expert can almost ignore these. Our job is then to plant objects that either totally mask what's below, or have an unusual pattern and are therefore investigated.

The masking pattern is first. While it is true that deep-detectors have modes that will ignore mineralized soil (occurs in nature, in rusty dump sites, in areas saturated with animal urine and waste, in salty areas, like where a salt lick was), any such masking will absorb some of the signal generated by a detector and therefore lower its efficiency. The organically created types of soil are easy to produce, but remember that searchers often start in dog pens and manure piles because that is where people bury their goods thinking that nobody would be willing to start there. To locate a naturally-occurring area, rent a metal detector and nose around a little yourself.

The artificially created array is more difficult, but research has turned up a few objects that seem to cause more problems than most. .22 caliber long rifle bullets (the complete loaded round) emerged as the object most likely to imitate the profile of a cache. These should be pushed into the ground using an iron rod that has the end drilled just big enough to accept the base of the round, and deep enough to allow only the nose to protrude. Once inserted to about a two foot depth, or deeper if possible, the rod is withdrawn and the loaded round stays. Iron nails also sound fairly close. Apparently a penny is too good a conductor and the sharp blip it produces is a dead give-away. The best way to utilize the penny is in a closely spaced array that masks what is underneath. The optimum spacing to foil deep-seekers is a grid with a penny every 4-6 inches. Pennies can be planted with an iron rod like the bullets, or by using a planting fid. Pennies dated earlier than 1983 will read stronger because of the greater copper content, so use these in a nuisance grid!

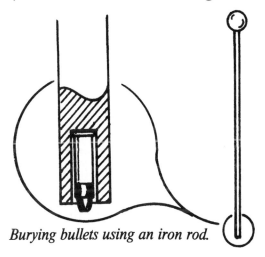

Burying bullets using an iron rod.

One other use for iron is that when searchers are using the super-sensitive PI-type detectors, or VLF-types that attempt to discriminate between junk and wanted targets, heavy use of ferrous particles will totally mask the ground below. This is an exception to the conductivity rule! To execute this mask, small bits of iron wire are also nice. The iron content in regular mineralized soil is roughly equivalent to that in a nail. Salt pellets sold for water softeners also make a good masking array because they can be scattered on the ground like seeds. Once the first few rains have dissolved them, they will register as signals, but cannot be dug out to allow a clear signal! Salt is very effective as an energy absorber and lowers detector efficiency, but may wreck a lawn, so use it in wooded areas only!

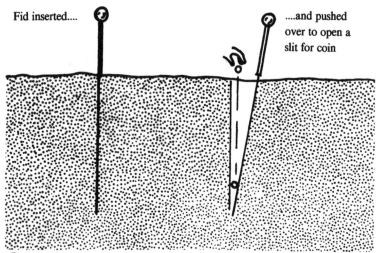

Fid inserted....   ....and pushed over to open a slit for coin

Some detectors also have trouble with bottlecaps.

Of course, actual junk targets can be buried but this is a lot of work! There is only one situation that calls for a false burial. If you suspect that non-law enforcement types may try to locate and dig up your cache, you should consider laying an active trap for them. In effect, you are committing yourself to breaking a lot of serious laws when you bury a container booby-trapped to explode when dug up and removed, but you might consider this necessary. Just consider that perfectly innocent people may inadvertently trigger such a device, or it may go off spontaneously. Beware of fuzzy thinking in this matter. It may be better to provide the cache with a nuisance device like a tear-gas or nausea-gas bomb. Such a device could be a standard part of all your legitimate caches, and wired or triggered in such a manner that only your informed handling would defuse the device. If you like this idea, consider using an explosive squib charge like a low-grade initiating cap surrounded by formaldehyde and wired to a battery and a microswitch fixed to the inside of the container, the contacts held open by the lid. Sawing or drilling through at a pre-measured place would allow defusing and easy re-sealing, if the container is needed again. Formaldehyde will jelly during long cold storage so cut it with alcohol. Another substance is chlor-acetone made by bubbling chlorine through acetone (nail polish remover). Eddie generates chlorine the quick and dirty way by pouring muriatic acid in with manganese dioxide. Chloracetone is actually a simple tear-gas compound and in liquid form will cause blindness if splashed into the eye, but it makes an area uninhabitable for a little while. Another possibility is a load of two dozen eggs or a twenty pound load of horse manure planted about a foot down as you fill your cache hole in. This may dissuade any further searching but remember that the horse manure will generate its own signal; the rotten eggs are better. A dead animal may also be a good bet.

Camouflage is often your best insurance against cache discovery. Eddie's favorite dodge is as follows. Obtain a dead cat or dog somewhere on the road. Roll it into an improvised body bag and then into a wooden crate. Now add a wooden plaque with the words, "Rest in Peace, Fluffy," or whatever, burned in with a woodburner, or done in magic marker. Add a couple of ribbons and a bag of small change and your decoy is ready. This little gem can be placed about a foot down and directly over a deep, important cache. The detector will get a positive signal (even with the sonar types), dig down, and come upon the grave of a beloved family pet. With a little luck, the coins will be considered the source of the signal and the animal covered up as before. This trick might also work with any piece of junk buried directly over the cache, like a typewriter, a coffee can, horseshoes, plow parts, tractor parts, wheel rim, box of tin cans, circular saw blade, etc. Just remember, the decoy will make it's own signal!

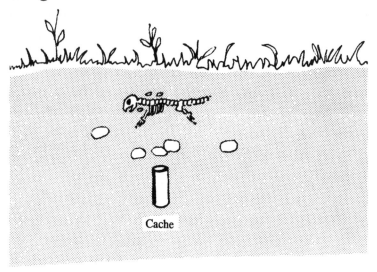

Cache

Another effective trick is a decoy cache container with inconsequential items like gasoline or food inside. The first cache located a foot down will be immediately stolen and the more valuable one located four feet down never detected.

Eddie also likes to put misleading labels in such caches, or even in real ones. The label says things like cache number four of five, when really there are twenty caches. A cute touch is to put a fake map of other cache locations in the dummy container, and arrange for the locations to be in difficult spots like under large rocks, in swamps, or in the next county. A false note, like "twenty m-16's under the old oak tree down ten feet," can really put a spark in the eye of a thief, but it will cure him double-quick when he goes excavating for such a treasure hoard.

There are some people who think that a large rock or other natural obstruction will deter seeking if it is placed directly over the cache, but there are problems with this. First off, one of the largest treasure finds in history happened because someone thought a large rock would make an effective barrier, while someone else who was looking thought the same thing! The rock became it's own landmark or attention-attractor. Secondly, it won't look natural for about three years if you plant a huge rock over a cache! If you try this trick, look for a flat naturally occurring rock and transplant it, keeping the depth the same. Felling a tree over the site may help (don't chop down a landmark) but it may be poached for firewood. A rotted stump is nice, if it looks natural and not dragged over. An old tangle of farmers' barbed wire or snow fence is excellent, as is a rusting thirty-nine Chevy or a refrigerator. Be imaginative!

So much for outfoxing the finders. The next chapter will discuss the methods to use when retrieving a cache for actual use.

HOW TO RETRIEVE
BURIAL CONTAINERS

Hold on! You're not just digging up that container to see if it's still buried there, are you? If you are, forget it! Consider this: it took you less than four hours to actually bury it, although the security precautions and the work to buy the goods took a lot longer. This means that in four hours anybody can be long gone with your container, and they won't know whose it is, probably wouldn't contact you anyway, and you can't report the theft of a full-auto weapon either. The only time you can catch thieves then is during the act, and it is impossible to patrol every four hours for the next six months. The bottom line is, either it's there or it's gone, and in either case digging for it won't help at all. Eddie recommends a check only every year or six months to verify that you can count on it being there in an emergency.

To perform routine checks like this, use *exactly* the same precautions you did when burying, since security is breached whenever you dig. In some cases, where the container must be destroyed to remove the contents, it is suitable to dig down close enough to probe for the cache, since no thief would remove the cache and leave a decoy in it's place. There is one important precaution, however, that applies whenever actually digging up a cache, not just checking. *Always Go Armed! Always Go Heavily Armed, and With Friends if Possible!* The reason is obvious: if you need this stuff, the times are a-changing and your cache is worth more than its weight in gold; it is worth life itself, perhaps several of them. To perform such a retrieval, try to deny access to the adjoining road with a few strategic roadblocks — trees down, stretched cable, booby trap, armed sniper team (one on each side of the road in concealment, and next to a lightweight roadblock like a six-inch tree trunk), or whatever you have. After access is secured and signals established for a breach of that security, proceed to the cache area and set up a series of observing posts to cover while you dig. The faster you do all of this, the better. Ideally it will take an hour and no more, and of course, go for the weapons cache first, food and gas next, then the incidentals. If your base is not secure, or is some distance away, leave the incidentals for another day.

Once the cache is unearthed, immediately break it down among the group and then split for transportation from the area. If there are several caches in the same section, remove all traces of the burial and containers, padding, wrapping, and whatever. The hole provides a good place for all of the above.

One other rule: don't ever use that site for a burial cache again; the risk is just too great.

ABOVE-GROUND CACHES

Law enforcement metal detectors are not just big frisbee-sized coils swung over the ground. The better models have interchangeable search coils and belt-mounted units that allow house and furniture construction searching in very tight corners. It is for this reason that above-ground caches should be either well-camouflaged and inaccessible, or located at some distance from your grounds and house.

Why cache above ground? Any low-security, low-loss/risk items should be stored this way. It increases accessibility and, quite frankly, you won't go out on a high-security burial to sock away thirty gallons of gasoline. This type of cache resists only the casual searcher, like a house thief.

A few good books have been written about constructing hidden compartments and false-bottoms for hiding, and Loompanics carries a good selection of these. It is a good bet, however, that the professionals also read these, so don't use any of the ideas straight from the books; modify them if at all possible. There is one advantage to an above-ground cache; it can be solidly constructed, bolted down and locked. Such a cache will be *immediately* metal-detected, but it cannot be easily ripped-off!

A shallow cache has a couple of advantages also. In cold climates it allows easy access, and can be just as easily re-packed. To construct such a cache, build or buy a wooden box sized to the article/s you want to store, dig a hole that size and about a foot and a half down. In the bottom of this hole, dig an additional trench and fill it with gravel or sand for drainage, kind of like constructing a little house-type basement or a foxhole.

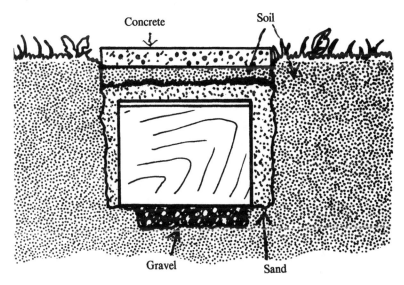

The wooden box is now coated with asphalt roofing compound or similar waterproofing and filled with packaged items. The top is secured with dowels and the hole covered with sand, using native soil the last four inches. It only takes about ten minutes to un-bury one of these. The ground above may also be covered with anything to deter casual access, like a trash barrel, a garden shed, your parked car, a kids' swimming pool — anything!

Caches in the house fall more in the area of hiding books, but a few comments are in order. Low-tech searching is done with a measuring tape. The outside of the suspect building is carefully dimensioned to determine if any hidden spaces exist. To avoid this approach look for spaces that are normally blank and inaccessible. A favorite space for Eddie is the space defined by a one-piece molded shower stall with a seat. A hatch through the adjoining wall to the below-seat area will allow at least two cubic feet of storage space, and the plumbing won't help detectors either.

Gasoline and water in particular are both good candidates for above-ground storage, for obvious reasons. Even though it is possible to preserve gas as outlined below, it is better to rotate your stock periodically, and in times of short supply (which usually precede times of *no* supply), it is hard not to dip into supplies in an emergency.

Gasoline has a few other things in it besides gas. In winter, a sophisticated form of dry-gas is blended in to prevent freeze-up. In all seasons other compounds are added to extend performance. Even the distillation process leaves some by-products. Ask anybody who stores a seasonally-used two-cycle engine (lawnmower, chain saw); the gas will turn to a gummy substance which clogs the carburetor needle orifice. To stabilize the chemical structure, several additives have been developed: phenylene diamine, aminophenol, L-13, and butylated hydroxytoluene. The best protection comes from 3.5 grains of butylated hydroxytoluene added per gallon, but seven or ten grains is permissible for longer time periods. One ounce equals 437.5 grains. For storage in excess of ten years, select a cool, dark spot, and add a slug of disodium EDTA (100 mg./gallon) to bond with free radical metal ions. Butylated hydroxytoluene (BHT) is used as a food preservative and can be obtained from vitamin companies, health food stores, and chemical supply houses. Two other considerations apply to gasoline storage: evaporation and contamination. The best, lowest cost storage is a 55-gallon drum. These come with a two-inch bung and a vent as well. Bury these in a hole large enough to allow a foot of clearance all around, and fill this space with screened sand. A variety of hand-operated pumps that can be attached to the bung are available from farm supply stores. Do not buy an electrically-operated pump, they require care in installation, and safety wiring, and won't operate in a crisis anyway! For safety, keep the drum dump a fifty foot minimum away from dwellings.

After making the installation, the first two or three batches of gasoline must be filtered because of possible contamination from rust particles, sand, or any foreign object. A particle five microns in diameter will damage the carburetor jet in an automobile! By contrast, a human hair is 100 microns in diameter. For regular filtering, manufacture a chamois separator, using chamois, which is available in most auto supply stores, as well as a large funnel with a wire strainer at the bottom. Just stretch the leather until it droops well into the funnel, putting some slack in the tie if necessary to gain clearance. Any trouble-causing particles will be filtered out. For the higher-performance engines in airplanes, a military filter-separator is required both to filter and dry high-test aviation gas. TM 5-4330-220-12 discusses suppliers of these units, or you can consult one of the newsstand aviation mags to find suppliers of these units, especially important to survivalists who have reserved slots in desert hideaway condos and require quick air transport there!

One last point: allow two inches of air space in a 55-gallon drum, for vapor expansion during temperature variations, or the drum will rupture! If your drums are not buried, but standing free, dig a ditch around the area to lead away the gas, as they do at large tank farms. Go visit one and look at the layout.

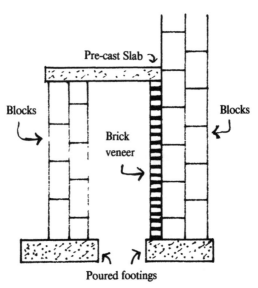

Machinery storage follows the same lines as for gun preservation, but due to the large size of most machines (lithographs for the resistance, generators) an accessible cache is mandatory. The best bet seems to be a room constructed to open into a basement. The reinforcement iron bar in some poured walls would be some aid to foxing metal detectors. With such a room, advance preparation is essential and extra iron could be added then!

BURIAL CONTAINERS: BUILT AND BOUGHT

Burial containers must have three features: imperviousness to water pressure/moisture, resistance to crushing earth, and resealability. The last item is important because it may be necessary to remove and replace a cache in times of emergency, and the original container *must* be reusable. Containers meeting all three needs can be built or bought. Let's look at the market first.

Three types of container are sold: (1) especially designed for survivalist/cache needs; (2) designed to seal and adaptable to cache requirements; and (3) sold because somebody thinks it will work, or thinks they can make *you* think it will work!

Eddie recommends several types, but tops on the list is the "Hide-a-vault" made by Monsanto and marketed by several firms. This is a one-piece, molded ABS plastic case with a screw-on cap. The "O" ring seal withstands water pressure to 20 PSI and the case is good for 78 foot pounds of impact. Dimensions are 6" x 12", shaped round. It comes with a wrench to screw on and off the end, and instructions. Obviously the size is good for small objects only, but for paper and gold/jewelry it is tops!

The next possibility is a plastic Nalgene bottle, made for the chemical laboratory trade. Sizes range from ounce to gallon, and the backpacker suppliers carry the medium sizes for liquids packing. To use, just fill, cap, wrap in a garbage bag and bury. Oddly enough, an ordinary plastic soft drink bottle (three sizes available) also works well if buried in sand-lined holes.

The five-gallon pails that fast-food restaurants get pickles and other foodstuffs in are also a favorite of the burial manual writers, but these must be carefully inspected to be sure the plastic seal is still intact and the lid/lip undamaged. These should be protected from mechanical damage by using a foam-lined hole. Larger polyethylene containers are also available industrially in 30- and 55-gallon sizes. Find these where you can; the magazines sometimes offer these for sale, but prices are lower when salvaging from local companies. *Beware* of containers that may have held poisonous chemicals, like fertilizers, insecticides, solvents, and so on. Cleaning these may be impossible, so ask about previous contents. Farmers buy pesticides in 5-gallon poly carboys and leave them empty in the field, but cleaning is tough.

Zip-lock and similar bags can be used if placed in a mechanically strong box, but this is not great protection.

The *Shotgun News* and similar papers also offer a wide variety of government surplus containers designed to hold everything from 8″ howitzer rounds to LAWs to whatever. They may be advertised well, but unless they are specifically designed to be buried, there is no guarantee of their reliability. It would take four days to rust a fine weapon in a damp container and you'll have a mess in the cold, cold ground.

One army surplus container of proven reliability is the ammo storage container, whether 30. cal, 50. cal, or other sizes. These have strong construction, waterproof gaskets, and good closures. There is only one drawback — it's all metal and shows up *well* on a metal detector. But in the right spot, it will serve.

The Cadillac of the burial containers is, of course, the plastic plumbing stock with end closures. A wide variety of material is available: polyethylene, polyvinyl chloride (PVC), ABS — all are useful.

PVC comes as high-head or low-head (different pressure ratings), in sizes from ¾" to 16" diameter, in 20 foot lengths, but some stores will cut it down for you. Farm suppliers have the best deals, since the pipe is used for tiling crop fields. They also carry the fitting for neat end closures. The low-head pipe will only accommodate fittings that glue on, so the high-head is recommended for screw-type closures, but it is *very* expensive. To put on either type of closure, special PVC glue is applied. Use the slow-setting glue or risk a hernia getting the parts aligned before they "freeze." Two types of screw closure are possible, either a male adapter with a threaded female cap or a female adapter with a threaded male insert. The first strategy is a little cheaper in parts prices.

To construct a set of PVC casings, assemble all the necessary end parts and make sure they fit your pipe size. Use a radial-arm saw to cut the pipe to the desired length — a plywood blade is best. Before gluing the pipe surface, dry-fit the adapters and mark with pencil where the adapter stops, then roughen the pipe up to this line, using a file, sandpaper (80 garnet), or a wire brush (fast). Now apply a generous coating of cement and apply the adapter, rotating it, as if screwing it on, at least a full turn. This eliminates air bubbles. A tap on the adapter with a rubber mallet will ensure a tight fit. Do *not* use the same glue as a sealant on the threaded end cap. The same procedure is followed if low-head pipe is used with glue-on ends.

There are alternate ways to seal the ends. Some plans recommend plexiglass circles, but these have a *poor* seal. Eddie recommends two ways: silicone caulking compound or epoxy/fiberglass. A large plug of either, or sealing around some other plug, like a wooden dowel or even a soft drink bottle, is effective.

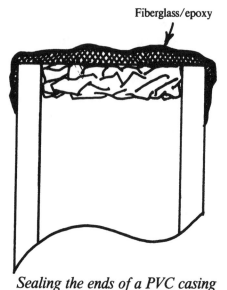

Fiberglass/epoxy

Sealing the ends of a PVC casing

The polyethylene pipe available is very difficult to seal, but it is inexpensive and very tough. The best seal is a tight-fitting, tapered, wooden plug jammed in *past* the mouth of the pipe about one inch, with epoxy poured in the space between the plug and the lip of the pipe. If epoxy is poured in from the other side as well, security is doubled. The poly can be heated up with a propane torch and "folded" over the cap for even more security.

The ABS plastic pipe is more expensive, but much stronger. Use this for the ultimate burial container for your AR-15. No amount of penny-pinching is worth such a fine weapon.

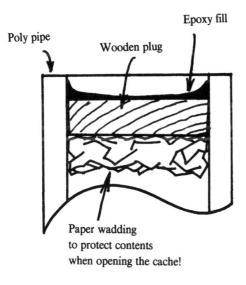

Epoxy fill

Poly pipe

Wooden plug

Paper wadding
to protect contents
when opening the cache!

For wooden crates, pallet wood makes a fine choice, or rough-sawn, air-dried hardwood. Any nails used in construction will show up, so use dowels to assemble such a box. Fluted or spiral-cut dowels are best, and the adhesive of choice is Weldwood brand plastic resin glue. This must be carefully mixed with water by volume, but it is waterproof and strong. Hardware stores stock dowels and glue. In a shallow cache a few nails will not matter however.

One type of container nobody seems to like is the home or precast concrete type. The precast ones are called septic tanks. They come in one or two pieces and have a wedge-shaped access hatch just large enough for a man. Eddie has been inside one; there is enough space in the 1500-gallon ones to store enough food and supplies for six months, or even a couple of people, in a pinch! Septic tanks are also being manufactured in molded plastic as well. You might consider putting a waterproof cache container in your own septic tank on a stout monofilament line, but remember: the feds know these tricks also! Obviously setting such a tank requires a backhoe.

The home-cast variety can take any shape you want. A favorite ploy is placing the access hatch below a paving stone in the garden, or a sod plug with a wire handle. A trip to the building supplier/brick and block supplier will turn up vitrified clay flue liners, clay tiles, specialty concrete blocks — all kinds of containers. Take your pick and lay it up. Epoxy-based concrete is available for specialty patching purposes, and a small sack of this can make the seal between a tile and a concrete bottom slab. Also pick up some crushed rock for drainage.

INFORMATION SECURITY

Documentation of what is stored, how it is stored, and where it is stored will be extensive, and any fragment of it is a dead giveaway of your operation. You need a code or a stash for the documents, and a safe-deposit box is a poor choice because of limited access by you and unlimited access by a warrant. The feds are also good at codes, after practice with those of bookies and numbers runners. The tough ones are sent to the FBI for solution, and the toughest of these go to the NSA where the employees solve them during the lunch hour! Nevertheless, a code is the best solution and here is how to do it. The Yellow Pages will list suppliers who will rent or lease you a pc-compatible computer and software; a store may even rent you some time! The software program you need is called Superkey and is published by Borland. It is extremely common in the industry. One of the functions of this program is an encryption/decryption subroutine that implements the DES algorithm, a sort of government standard for code security, although it has been watered down from its original form. We will fix that!

The information must be typed into the computer as a file, and any word processor/text editor is suitable for that job. Get the rentee to describe exactly what you need to do to make it work, and then let him watch while you try the whole procedure with a dummy file! Once the file is complete, run it through the superkey encryption process using whatever keyword you can absolutely remember, since if you forget the key, the informtion is *absolutely, forever, and completely lost!* The trick to restoring perfect security to the encryption is to encode it *twice* with different keywords. One little note: do not rename the file after encryption or the data will be scrambled. Also, use the text-only mode of encoding. After the dry-run, leave and come back later in the week when nobody will look over your shoulder. Now key in the real data, your cache locations and lists, and encrypt it as before. If you are wary of computers, make a copy of the unencoded file, and a copy of the encoded file as well, and store them in such a manner that improper opening of the container they are in will destroy them. In other words, booby-trap the hiding place. Remember to make a printout of the file so it can be rekeyed into another computer and decoded if worst comes to worst.

Now the data is safe and secure, and your job is done. Congratulate yourself, because you are better off than 99.4 percent of your fellow beings, and if you need help in an emergency, you know where to find it.

Another code to consider if you don't like computers, is a book code. Each character of the cache data is located, one at a time, in a book, and the page number, line, word and position in the word is noted down as the encoded plaintext. To decode, simply get a copy of the book and reconstruct the original list one character at a time. The security is in knowing which book (and edition), so pick something out of the ordinary, like *The Use and Abuse of the Recriprocating Steam Boiler.* Book codes are very secure, and some have never been broken!

That's all for burying things. Be sure to check out Eddie's fine series on lock picking and making lockpicking tools, also available from Loompanics. Hang 'em high and bury 'em deep.

APPENDIX: SOURCE LISTINGS

Survival Food

Oregon Freeze Dry Foods Inc.
PO Box 1048
Albany, OR 97321

Sterling H. Nelson and Sons Inc.
PO Box 1296
Salt Lake City, UT 84110

W. Atlee Burpee Co.
Dept. CFC
Warminister, PA 18974

Clyde Robin
PO Box 2091
Castro Valley, CA 94546

Manufactured Burial Containers

Jolly Roger Surplus Company
PO Box 7012
Van Nuys, CA 91409

Jolly Roger Surplus Company
PO Box 53
Roxbury, PA 17251

Jerry's Barrels
Rt. 1 Box 573
Greenville, MS 38701

Glenns Trading Post
Poverty Flat
PO Box 857 Dept ASG
Edgar, AZ 85925

Sherwood Distributing Inc.
18714 Parthenia St.
Northridge, CA 91324

Better Safe
Box 428
Dufur, OR 97021

Shotgun News
PO Box 669
Hastings, NB 68901

SI Equipment
PO Box 4727
Carson, CA 90749

GRD Supplies
PO Box 3041
San Diego, CA 92103

Brigade Quartermasters Ltd.
266 Roswell St.
Marietta, GA 30060-9988

Continental Supply
20 Griffith Lane
Ridgefield, CT 06877

Dessicants

Nasco Inc.
PO Box 643
E. Greenwich, RI 02818

Sargent-Welch
7300 No. Linder Ave.
Skokie, IL 60076

Hydrosorbent Co.
PO Box 675
Rye, NY 10580

Key Products (VA-PO-TEX)
PO Box 601
La Canada, CA 91011

Survival, Inc.
PO Box 2246
Culver City, CA 90230

VWR Scientific
PO Box 3200

Rincon Annex
San Francisco, CA 94119

Cosmoline

Southwestern Arms Co. Inc.
Rt. 28, Box 84A
Milford, NY 13807

B.W. Trading Co.
Box 692-1016
Newark, OH 43055

Gene Lightsey
559 Park Terrace
Birmingham, AL 35226

Publications

Gun Week
PO Box 150
Sidney, OH 45365

Loompanics Unlimited
PO Box 1197
Port Townsend, WA 98368

Plastic Coatings

Cope Plastics
1111 W. Selmar
Godfrey, IL 62035

Dipseal Plastics
2311 23rd Ave.
Rockford, IL 61101

Plasti-Dip International
1458 West Country Road C
St. Paul, MN 55113

Fuel Preservative

Student Service Inc.
622 W. Colorado St.
Glendale, CA 91204

Ammunition Information

S.A.A.M.I.
420 Lexington Ave.
New York, NY 10017